ON THE INCARNATION FOR TEENS

ON THE INCARNATION FOR TEENS

by

Aidan McLachlan

ST SHENOUDA PRESS
SYDNEY, AUSTRALIA
2018

On the Incarnation for Teens

ST SHENOUDA PRESS
8419 Putty Rd,
Putty, NSW, 2330

www.stshenoudapress.com

ISBN 13: 978-0-6482814-5-0

About the Author:

Aidan McLachlan is an Australian-Egyptian who serves at St Mark's Coptic Church Sydney, Australia. He is currently studying Medicine at the University of New South Wales and undertaking his postgraduate studies at St Cyril's Coptic Orthodox Theological College.

Cover Design:
Mariana Hanna
In and Out Creation Pty Ltd
inandoutcreations.com.au

Interior Design:
Hani Ghaly,
Begoury Graphics
begourygraphics@gmail.com

CONTENTS

INTRODUCTION

St Athanasius wrote this book, 'On the Incarnation', not as a book but as a letter. It was the second letter addressed to his friend, Makarios, who had previously been pagan but was being catechised to Christianity. In the first letter, he spoke of the foolishness of pagan idols and encouraged Makarios to continue his Christian journey. Having spoken about why pagans were wrong, he now needed to write about why Christians were right. To do this, he sought to describe one of the greatest mysteries of the Church: The Incarnation.

St Athanasius describes what he calls a "divine dilemma", which means "God's big problem." It was that God had made man for life but instead man had chosen death. God had said at the beginning "In the day that you eat of [that tree] you shall surely die" (Genesis 2:17) and man had foolishly eaten of the tree. What was God to do? Could He

People, Places &Things

Bishop or Pope of Alexandria

When people hear 'Pope', which means 'Father', they think of the Pope in Rome. However, in the early church the title wasn't for him alone. The Bishop of Alexandria was also called Pope. The first recorded usage of Pope for the Bishop of Alexandria was Pope Heraclas of Alexandria who was bishop from 227-240 AD. To this day, the current Bishop of Alexandria still uses this title (Pope Tawadros II). Pope comes from a Coptic word 'Papas' meaning 'Father' and shows the closeness of the Bishop to his flock.

simply leave man to die? That couldn't be an option, He had made man out of love, and that would be unloving. Could He go back on His word? That also wouldn't work because He would make Himself a liar and that's simply impossible! Long story short the only solution, St Athanasius tells us, is that the problem could only be solved in the incarnation of 'His Word,' that is Jesus Christ His Son.

This discussion forms the bulk of the book.

After that, St Athanasius wasn't actually done debating in his previous letter, and so he goes on to debate firstly with the Jews. Using the Old Testament, he argues that Jesus Christ is the Messiah that is spoken about that would fulfil the Scriptures. After debating with the Jews, Athanasius debates with the Gentiles to show them why Christ is the Saviour of the world and why Christianity is true.

Catechumens

What does 'catechise' mean? Who were the 'catechumens'? Catechism comes from a Greek word meaning 'to teach'. Someone who underwent 'catechism' was called a 'catechumen'. These were people who decided that they wanted to learn more about Christianity. After they had been taught about Christianity, they were baptised and could partake of the Eucharist.

Before they were baptised, catechumens were asked to exit the church halfway through the Liturgy before the priest began to consecrate the Gifts. To this day, the first half of the liturgy is called 'The Liturgy of the Catechumens' and the second half 'The Liturgy of the Faithful.'

One of the most famous quotes from St Athanasius' book is: "He [Jesus Christ] was incarnate, that we might be made god." This is repeated later by some of the Fathers as "He became man that we might become god." This is scary language! What do you mean we might become god? In summary, this is the central belief of the Christian life: that we must do as Jesus has done that we may be like Him by God's grace. Onwards, to the book!

REFLECTION

St Athanasius went through all this effort for his friend, and look at the fruit that came from it - an absolute masterpiece which has touched so many people's lives and understanding over the centuries. So what can you today for a friend to make a difference to their lives and to their faith? Don't forget that what you do today can have a ripple effect and make a difference to someone tomorrow.

CHAPTER ONE

THE PROLOGUE

The book begins with the prologue. Here St Athanasius wants to make sure that his friend, Makarios, is up to date with what's been said in his previous letter, Against the Gentiles. Firstly, he mentions that man has invented idols and that in his corruption man has chosen to worship these invented idols (unlike the Living God of Abraham, Isaac, and Jacob who in fact invented man!). Secondly and importantly, he declares that the Word of the Father (i.e. Jesus Christ) is the one who made and organised the world.

Apart from a reminder, the opening chapter is an invitation: "Come now, blessed one and true lover of Christ, let us, with the faith of our religion, relate also the things concerning the Incarnation of the Word and expound His divine manifestation to us, which the Jews slander and the Greeks mock, but we ourselves venerate..." From the beginning, Athanasius invites us to learn but also to recognise that what we're about to learn is often what we hear other people mock, what we're about to learn is often what we hear other people describe as ridiculous, and yet what we're about to learn is not according to the ways of man but to the ways of God. "With men this is impossible, but with God all things are possible." (Matthew 19:26).

Now time for some important information that we need to keep in mind as we read. This Word of the Father, we have to recall, is not human by nature. That means

CHAPTER ONE

He was not always so but because of His love for humanity, He became human to save us. Furthermore, He was the one that made the world, so it makes perfect sense that He should come and save it to restore it to how it ought to be.

WHAT THE SCRIPTURES SAY:

At the beginning of the Gospel of St John, he writes "In the beginning was the Word, and the Word was with God, and the Word was God." (John 1:1). This Word, we know to be Jesus Christ and often St Athanasius, like many of the Fathers, will just write 'The Word of God'. St Athanasius constantly talks about man being 'logical' or 'rational' which is actually a play on words! He's trying to say not only that man's smart, but also that he's in the image of God who is the Logos (logical/logos) Importantly, it means that Christ and the wisdom of His Church should be our Logic. He should be the One we turn to when we need to make a decision.

REFLECTION

How much does it bother us that others disagree with us like many of the Jews and the Greeks disagreed with the early Christians? It can make us sad, scared, angry, and many more. Isn't it then very important that we all search for the truth? And what is Truth but Jesus Christ? As He says "I am the Way, the Truth, and the Life" (John 14:6)

ST ATHANASIUS

'On the Incarnation', one of the most famous books in all Christian history, was written by an equally famous saint – beloved of the Egyptians – St Athanasius the Great of Alexandria. Athanasius was born around 299 AD. At a young age he was noticed by Alexander, the bishop of Alexandria, play-acting the liturgy with other children where he acted as the priest. The Synaxarium*, which is the Church's collection of the stories of the saints, claims that Bishop Alexander saw him and said, "This child will be in a great position one day."

Sure enough, St Athanasius went on to live life to the fullest. He was taken under Bishop Alexander's wing and became his deacon. At a very young age (around 26), Athanasius had a major role in the Council of Nicaea* of 325 where he defended Christianity from the arguments of the Arian heretics. These were followers of an Egyptian priest called Arius who famously claimed that "there was a time when the Son was not." What this meant was that Arius believed that the Son, Jesus Christ, did not exist from the beginning of time and thus was not God. Seeing

People, Places &Things

Council of Nicaea

The Council of Nicaea was called in 325 AD by the Roman emperor Constantine to solve a doctrinal fuss and bring the church back into unity. At the end of the council, with thanks to St Athanasius, they made a Creed (a word which kind of means 'what I believe'). This Creed, which was established over one and a half thousand years ago (and tidied up by another council in Constantinople in 381), is still recited in the Church today. Can you remember it all?

the danger in this and seeing that the very fact of our salvation through Christ was in jeopardy, Athanasius successfully argued against him and became a hero of the Church. This was to cause him much difficulty for the rest of his life. As Socrates (380-439) the Church historian writes, "Athanasius' fluency in speech and his outspokenness in the council of Nicaea brought over him all the hardships that he encountered in his life."

A few years after this council, in 328, Athanasius was made Bishop of Alexandria by the people*. He was Bishop for 46 years, making him one of the longest to hold the See of St Mark. However, his life was constantly troubled by the Arians. They made false accusations against Athanasius to the emperor and, through flattery and deceit, managed to convince him to exile Athanasius. This happened five times in his life and he spent 17 of his 46 years as Bishop of Alexandria in exile. While in exile, he made many important friends including St Anthony the Great, Father of the monks, and Athanasius learned much from him.

Athanasius wrote many books, three of which are particularly famous. The first is called 'Against the Gentiles' where he argues against the pagans, the second is 'On the Incarnation,' where he speaks about the incarnation of Jesus Christ, and the third is 'The Life of St Anthony', where he tells the story of the great monk St Anthony. Because of his constant rivalry with emperors, Athanasius earned the Latin title

Synaxarium

After the reading of the Acts of the Apostles, the Synaxarium is read. Synaxarium comes from the Greek word meaning 'to bring together' as it brings together the stories of saints who have gone before, and in doing this brings us together and closer to God. Interestingly, while we usually celebrate each other's birthdays, with saints we instead celebrate a saint on the day he/she died! How can we understand this? If we look at a letter written by St Ignatius of Antioch (35-107 AD) to the Romans, he says of his impending martyrdom: "The time of my birth is at hand." For this saint, his martyrdom and death, were his birthday with Christ. So we do celebrate the saints' birthdays, just a slightly different kind of birth.

'Athanasius Contra Mundum' which means 'Athanasius Against the World'. Because of his contribution to Christian theology, Athanasius earned the Coptic title 'Athanasios Pi-Apostolikos' which means 'Athanasius the Apostolic.' This famous saint was reposed in the Lord on the 2nd of May, 373 AD (the 7th of Bashons, 89 AM) when the Church still celebrates his feast.

REFLECTION

At such a young age it was clear that St Athansius would have a part to play in leading the church, when he was seen play-acting part of the liturgy. This would have been because he immersed himself in the life of the church. This opportunity is open to all of us if we likewise immerse ourselves in the life of the church and become active members.

CHAPTER TWO

THE DIVINE DILEMMA PART I (LIFE AND DEATH) [2-10]

[2] Now the book has begun properly. St Athanasius doesn't want to miss anything, so he starts right from the beginning: the creation of the world. In order to do this, he needs to compare the Christian teaching of creation to many of the philosophers of his time.

First are the Epicureans, so called as they are the followers of Epicurus. They, like many people nowadays, believed that the world came about spontaneously. But, St Athanasius writes, how can we then explain the obvious order of the universe? He says, "Such order indicates that they did not come into being spontaneously, but shows that a cause preceded them, from which one can apprehend the God who ordered and created all things." In other words, by this order we can determine that there must be someone who is doing all this ordering, and that someone is God.

Second are the Platonists, followers of the famous Athenian philosopher Plato. They believed that God didn't make matter at all, He simply arranged it. But there are a few problems with that too: saying that God didn't make matter suggests that He couldn't make matter and thus lacks skill. Surely no one would say that about God! Secondly, how could you call God the Creator or the Maker if He didn't actually create or make? And so we

CHAPTER TWO

have to throw out the Platonists' teaching as well.

The last people that Athanasius had to correct are a group of heretics who claimed that they believed in the Bible, but that there was another who created the universe who wasn't God. Yet, this is in direct contradiction of the Bible itself which says, "All things were made through Him and without Him nothing was made that was made" (John 1:3). They must be wrong too! So what is right?

REFLECTION

There were so many thoughts and opinions that were circulating at the time, and you can only imagine how confusing it would have been. But it's interesting to see that St Athanasius found his grounding in the Scriptures. Likewise for us today, there are many thoughts and opinions which attempt to sway us every which way, about so many different issues. But based on St Athanasius' example we learn to always refer to the Scriptures to guide us and direct us in our lives.

[3] Knowing what is wrong, it will be easier to understand what is right. St Athanasius teaches us the true teaching of creation guided by "the inspired teaching", which is of course the Holy Scriptures. That teaching is that God made the world out of nothing.

Summing up the argument so far, St Athanasius says that "For [the Bible] knows that neither spontaneously, as it is not without providence, nor from pre-existent matter, as God is not weak, but from nothing and having absolutely no existence God brought the universe into being through the Word." God is the source of all goodness, and, overflowing with goodness, He made all of creation through His Word (that's why He said 'it was good' in Genesis 1!). What's more, the crown of all of His creation was mankind, whom He made to bear His own image and thus be rational, unlike the animals. Furthermore, in making man rational He gave man his own will – free will – but he saw that this could be a problem: man could choose whatever he wanted, good or evil. To try to prevent evil and draw man to good (that is, God), He gave them a law: if man lived a good life directed to God and directed to loving God he may remain in paradise; if he chose evil, and if he became wicked, he would die (Genesis 1:27) and remain in corruption.

[4]. At this point, the reader may think "Wait a second, I thought this book was about the Incarnation? Why are we getting this big

history lesson?" St Athanasius tells us that if we don't understand this history – the history of salvation – we will not understand why God came to us in the body of a man at all, "in the form of a slave" (Phil 2:7). It is only when we understand why God needed to come that we can understand His great love for mankind

St Athanasius continues to say that man was made for immortality and for incorruption. But we remember that God made everything from nothing, so everything – of course including man – derives its existence from God. When man decided to turn away from God, he turned away from existence and from Life itself, and started to die. Like when someone closes their eyes to the light they no longer sees light, so too did man close his eyes and his heart to God.

WHAT THE SCRIPTURES SAY

St Athanasius quotes from Psalm 81: "I said you are gods, and all sons of the Most High; but you die like human beings and fall like any prince" (Psalm 81:6-7). We are gods! We are sons of the Most High! This is saying we were made by God to live for Him, but we die like human beings and fall. We turned away from life! This is the greatest tragedy that was ever heard.

[5]. So we know that man turned away from God and so brought death upon himself because God was the source of life. But why did man bring death upon himself?

How did he become subject to it? It is because he listened to the devil, instead of God. He chose evil instead of good. God had made man good and in communion with Him in the beginning. When man turned away from God, that is, from good and from life, man made the opposites: evil and death. These are not God's makings but are man's makings due to his rejectionon of God.

Man became more and more evil and so committed himself more and more to death. Like a snowball rolling down a snowy mountain gets bigger and bigger and rolls faster and faster, so too was man with his wickedness hurtling towards death. St Athanasius writes: "From the beginning they were inventors of evil and called death and corruption down upon themselves; while later, turning to vice and exceeding all lawlessness, not stopping at one evil but making in time every new evil, they became insatiable in sinning."

God had made man for incorruption and for immortality, but instead man had chosen the devil, destruction, and death.

People, Places &Things

In the Liturgy:

Does this all sound familiar? It should! We retell and remember this divine tragedy every time we go to the liturgy. The first words of the prayer of reconciliation prayed by the priest are "God, the Great and the Eternal, Who formed man in incorruption; and death which entered into the world by the envy of the devil..."

[6]. Here, St Athanasius has reached the heart of the problem, the 'Divine Dilemma'. God had established the law that if man should disobey Him then man will surely die. Man had disobeyed and was now subject to death. It seemed there was no way out, it seemed there were two wrong choices:

1. God could remove the law entirely so that man would not have to die. But if He did this then God would be made a liar, for He had said that if man transgressed the law then he would die. God cannot be a liar for He is not only true but Truth itself.

2. Alternatively, God could let man die but again this is improper of God. He had made man out of love and so letting him die would not be loving. It would also constitute a defeat at the hands of man's own negligence and the devil and his legion of demons. He might as well have not made man at all. Surely God could not allow this either.

What was God to do? This was the Divine Dilemma, the greatest challenge of the story of Salvation that bore the greatest solution in the story of Salvation.

[7]. Were these the only two options? St Athanasius thinks, what else could God do? What other options did He have?

Perhaps He could demand repentance from man? Would that be enough to save mankind? Unfortunately not. Repentance wouldn't satisfy the law that God had established (remember: if you disobey me, if you eat of the tree, you shall surely die). Also, St Athanasius says, while repentance can overcome the offence that sin had caused God and it can also direct man towards God, there was another problem. When man sinned, death entered his nature, and he became subject to death as the law declared. Repentance cannot change a man's nature. Only God, who made man, can fix man's nature. Man could not, and cannot, save himself on his own. He needed God's help and he needed it desperately – it was a matter of Life or death!

There was only One Who could help. This was the One Who had made the universe in the first place. Man needed the Maker's help since man had in part 'unmade' himself

REFLECTION

Don't go too fast, just because man can't save himself through repentance doesn't mean we shouldn't repent! Salvation is a 'synergy', which means 'working together'. Man must work together with God. Man does only a small part in the work compared to what God does, but it is still important. One of the things man can do to work with God is repent. How often do you repent with a priest or in your own prayers? What are other ways you can work with God?

by sinning – he had turned away from God who was the source of his life and existence, and consequently lost part of his life and existence. This One Who could help was the Word of the Father.

[8]. St Athanasius describes the carnage that God watched over: the excessive wickedness of man, man's destruction of each other, man's destruction of himself, and man's submission to death. He saw this, and it was not good. So, what was his solution? "He takes for Himself a body and that not foreign to our own." How wondrous to read? How marvellous to tell? God the great, God the eternal and unchanging, God the uncontainable and indescribable, took on a body and with it our corrupted humanity. What a great mystery!

Importantly, St Athanasius says, He didn't simply appear in a body or wish to be in a body but He took on our very humanity in all its corruption having formed it "as a temple" from a Virgin, that is St Mary.

But why did Christ do this? What did He accomplish in doing this?

Firstly, taking a body out of pure love for all of mankind and delivering it willingly up to death he fulfilled the law that God had set. For the law required the death of man who sinned, but God – in whom all men exist, since He made them all – could therefore die on behalf of all of mankind. So He became Man and died for mankind. Since He had made

What Saint Athanasius Said

"For this purpose, then, the incorporeal and incorruptible and immaterial Word of God comes into our realm, although He was not formerly distant. For no part of creation is left void of Him; while abiding with his own Father, He has filled all things in every place."

mankind, He could die for all of mankind.

Secondly, mankind had made the body corrupt. The Word of God took on the body so that by putting on the body in all its weakness and death, He could give it His life which is manifest in the Resurrection. He could thus turn man, in his corruption, back towards incorruption.

Notice that St Athanasius can explain why this happened, why Christ had to take on a body and save us but he never tries to explain how it happened, how God who is infinite, could fit in a body that is finite. This is one of the greatest mysteries of the Christian teaching.

[9]. Now God couldn't simply fulfil the law just as He was because, being God, He is immortal. He therefore had to take on our corrupted bodies so that He could purify them. St Athanasius says that firstly He was 'above all', being the Son of God and therefore being able to abolish the law. Then He became

People, Places &Things

Baptism

The Mystery of Baptism is related to this very act! St Paul writes "Or do you not know that as many of us as were baptized into Christ Jesus were baptized into His death?" (Romans 6:3). Baptism allows us to take part in Christ's conquering of death, in Christ's fulfilling the law, in Christ's restoration of humanity! St Paul continues to say "Therefore we were buried with Him through baptism into death, that just as Christ was raised from the dead by the glory of the Father, even so we also should walk in newness of life." (Romans 6:4) 'with all' so that we too could participate in His trampling over death because we are like Him. He came down to us, to bring us up to Him!

Apart from being very wise, St Athanasius is also an eloquent author. He describes Christ's Incarnation as like when a Great King comes into a city and builds his castle in it. Since the King is present no bandit or enemy is able to attack it and the city is worthy of great honour and worthy of the greatest care. Just like this, Christ's coming into our realm has conquered the final enemy, which is death, and no longer does corruption hold power over us. Had He not come, mankind would have certainly perished.

[10]. Continuing his metaphor of the king, St Athanasius says that we are in God's kingdom. This kingdom was pillaged by bandits, by Satan, because of the

REFLECTION

How amazing is it know that we have the Creator of the world, the king of the castle, on our side. How can we ever worry? As weak humans we find that we still worry when we forget this fact. But we have to make an effort to remind ourselves daily of God's presence in our lives and of His absolute power over all. What can we do to bring this beautiful fact to our minds daily?

carelessness of its citizens. Yet it was not right for a righteous king to leave His subjects to be attacked, even though they had transgressed. Therefore, He looked past their weakness, so that they could focus on His honour.

St Athanasius then cites much of the Scriptures to argue his point: not only that Christ had died for all, but also that it was fitting that He should be the one to save mankind since He was the one that created mankind.

His conclusion is that after Christ's incarnation and glorious resurrection, no longer does man die in condemnation. Instead, man can die in hope of the resurrection. Yet there was another reason why the Word of God was incarnate...

WHAT THE SCRIPTURES SAY

"But we see Jesus, who was made a little lower than the angels, for the suffering of death crowned with glory and honour, that He, by the grace of God, might taste death for everyone. For it was fitting for Him, for whom are all things and by whom are all things, in bringing many sons to glory, to make the captain of their salvation perfect through sufferings" (Hebrew 2:9-10)

"For since by man came death, by Man also came the resurrection of the dead. For as in Adam all die, even so in Christ all shall be made alive." (1 Corinthians 15:21-22)

CHAPTER II SUMMARY

What happened in this chapter is as follows:

• In the beginning, God made man out of nothing and He made man in union with Him. He also made a law that if man were to choose evil (a concept of man's own making), then he would surely die.

• Man, lured by the devil, chose evil and became corrupted by death. Since he had turned away from Life, which is God Himself since God had made him from nothing, man introduced death into the world.

• God couldn't let man die because it was unworthy of Him, so He had to find a way to rescue man from his corrupted nature.

• The only option for God due to His love for us was the incarnation; the Word of God must take on a corrupt body so that He could fulfil the law that had been broken and bring the fullness of life back to corrupted man.

CHAPTER THREE

CHAPTER THREE

THE DIVINE DILEMMA PART II

[11]. To understand the next dilemma that God had, again St Athanasius looks back to Creation. When God made man, He made him out of nothing. Therefore, man was created while God was uncreated. God had also made man with a body – he was 'corporeal' (this just means 'having a body'), while God is 'incorporeal' ('not having a body'). Because of these two huge differences, man wasn't able to know God, as God is on a completely different plane.

In order to counteract this and because God loved us so much that He wanted us to know Him, man was made in God's image. This way, by knowing God, man could live the truly blessed and happy life. But man, that woeful creature, turned his face from God and corrupted that image and that nature. Forgetting the true God, they fashioned gods for themselves out of wood and stone. Yet these gods are so foolish when compared to the true and living God. So, man lost his nature. Since he was made in the image of God the Logos, who is rationality and truth itself, man became irrational and was like the animals. He made magical arts, set up idols, and devised ways of discerning truth from the stars and heavenly bodies, instead of the truly heavenly.

God had never hidden Himself, man had closed his eyes to God and forgotten Him, being caught instead by the gods and idols of his own making, and of the world around him. This was a second dilemma for God, how could man know God now that he had corrupted his nature so greatly?

WHAT THE SCRIPTURES SAY:

St Paul saw this corruption of man as well and wrote that man "Serves the creature rather than the Creator, who is blessed forever. Amen." (Romans 1:25). Everything that was made is made by God and so, when there is anything praiseworthy in the world, it makes no sense to praise it unless it leads us to praising God.

REFLECTION

How often do we set up our own idols? How often do we serve things that aren't God, like our hunger, our own interests, or our desires? Do we not then become like foolish and primitive man who turned away from God in the first place? How greatly are we corrupting our hearts by doing this?

[12]. God, knowing everything, foresaw that man would turn away from Him. So he tried to offer man clues, reminders, and hints that He is their Maker. There were many of these and they all revealed God's unending and unquenchable love for mankind:

• First, we saw God made man in the image of Himself so that man might see his fellow man and together look up to God. Yet man's sin corrupted that nature and so man failed to see God in his brother.

• Then, He made beautiful creation, a place man could rest his head and call home. Surely this would be enough for man to look upwards to God. Yet this was not enough for man, and he turned creation into idols.

• God did not give in and so He sent man the law and the prophets so that if man were not able to look up and see the beauty of the heavens he could learn from holy men who were his fellow brother, how to also be holy. Yet man killed the prophets and disobeyed the laws.

Despite these promptings, man continued to feast on evil and to satisfy himself with his own lusts and wicked ways. No longer did he appear rational – like the Word of God who is Himself reason – but he became irrational.

[13]. Here again is the problem: man had been made to be in communion with God yet by the devil's deceit man had turned away

from God. He had gone so far from God that he no longer could recognise God. What was God to do? Man had been made to live the rational life but instead was living the irrational life. It would have been better for God to have made man irrational and let him be an animal, but He hadn't and He couldn't leave His creation to be corrupted by sin and death.

St Athanasius again uses an analogy: if a King had a piece of land, He wouldn't leave the people to think they serve some other, especially not one that would destroy them. Instead He would ensure they know Him, He would contact them by letters, He would be amongst them that they may know who gave them their livelihood. How much more then would this be the case for God who gave man life?

There was only one option for God, He must restore the man to be in His image and to save him from corruption, so that man could be in communion with God again. There was only one way this could be accomplished, only one Person that could save man. The Word of God. The Son of the Father. Jesus Christ Himself.

Man couldn't recover the lost image since he had lost the image and did not know what the image was of, nor could angels since they were not even images at all. Only the Word could accomplish this, by taking on the body and death and by revealing to mankind the Image of the Father that man had forgotten.

WHAT THE SCRIPTURES SAY:

St Paul writes of Christ, "He is the image of the invisible God, the firstborn over all creation." (Colossians 1:15). Christ is the Image of the Father and through Him we know the Father as St John the Evangelist writes "No one comes to the Father except through Me" (John 14:6)

[14]. In order for us to be able to understand this, St Athanasius uses another analogy: think of a piece of canvas upon which a portrait was painted. If by someone's wicked actions this canvas was made dirty and the portrait was no longer clearly visible, then the one who is in the portrait would have to come again that it may be repainted. Yet the canvas itself is valuable simply because this portrait was on it and so cannot be thrown away. In this way, the Word needed to come again that man may see the image more clearly.

REFLECTION

Do you ever search for God's work in your own day? If you never search for God, how do you expect to find Him? How do you know that He hasn't been revealing Himself to you in your fellow man, in the beauty of His creation, or in His holy people if you don't look?

Here St Athanasius says that being 'reborn' is crucial so that we can take on the image again (we can think of it as being 'repainted'), and where does this happen? Of course, in baptism. Doesn't it make sense now why we think it is so important?

Now man could still not perceive God through the inhabited world since it was corrupted by idolatry and evil. How was man to cleanse the window of the universe and find God through it if he was not able to look past the demons that blocked his view, or was not even able to see God at all? Perhaps a holy man was needed? But even a holy man falls victim to the same traps. Surely someone greater than man – or more than 'just a man' – was needed. It was the incarnated, the made-into-man, Word of God that was needed for He sees God and can show man God.

REFLECTION

Do we ever see God acting in other people through their kindness? Do we give thanks to God when we see this kindness or do we just thank the person (if that)? Do we ever let God work through us?

Also, how amazing is it to think that God is a painter and we are His canvas. The question is, will we give God an opportunity to finely paint us into His image, or will we let the world take up space on our canvas with its random splashes that distort the canvas?

"If they were struck by creation, yet they saw it confessing Christ as Lord; or if their minds were predisposed towards human beings, such that they supposed them gods, yet comparing the works of the Saviour with theirs, the Saviour alone among human beings, appeared the Son of God, for there were no such works among them as done by the God Word; and if they were predisposed towards the demons, yet seeing them put to flight by the Lord, they knew that only He was the Word of God and that the demons were not gods."

[15]. St Athanasius again uses his literary flair and describes God as a teacher. Teachers are often much brighter than their students and yet, because they love their students (or God does at least), they are willing to use simpler methods to teach things to their students. In the same way, since man forgot how to understand with his heart but instead only understood with his senses, God descended to reveal himself in a body so that man could understand Him with his senses. Before God was described as a painter, emphasising the beauty of the world as God's creation. Here God is described as a teacher, emphasising His wisdom.

Now that man has seen God in the flesh, he is able to see things more clearly for the Word of God has led man from Himself to consider His Father. All the things that man thought wonderful before are now insignificant compared to God or are made more wonderful because they are God's!

If man loved the beauty of the created world, He loved it all the more because it revealed God's handiwork. If man thought that the works of human beings are great, they are now insignificant when compared to the wonders done by God the Word. If man was lured to demonic ways, they became weak and worthless when they were put to flight by the Lord. If man was obsessed with past fallen heroes and noblemen, now they paled in comparison to the heroic one who overcame death.

Though we find many things that we think are great in our lives, God is far greater. The things that are actually great in our lives are this way because of God's making them so! This is another reason why Christ was incarnated as a human being: that He may draw man from the foolery he had fallen into and lead him to the Father.

Though we find many things that we think are great in our lives, God is far greater. The things that are actually great in our lives are this way because of God's making them so! This is another reason why Christ was incarnated as a human being: that He may draw man from the foolery he had fallen into and lead him to the Father.

REFLECTION

Does God enrich my life like St Athanasius describes? Do I give him an opportunity to do this? How can I try to see things as God's work and make them appear more wonderful? We're so lucky with all the things that God has blessed us with – whether that be family, friends, food or an education. But sometimes we fall in love with the gifts and forget the Giver. Sometimes we forget that although all these things are great, they are nothing when compared with the God who created them and gave them to us. One way we can avoid falling into the trap of forgetting who God is, is to not only thank God for what He gives, but to thank God for who He is, such as for being merciful, loving and kind.

[16]. Now we know another reason why the Word of God was incarnated: to remind man who God is and to draw man back to Him. St Athanasius says we learn something else: this is why Christ couldn't simply be incarnated, die, and resurrect invisibly. If He only needed to fulfil the law or purify man from corruption (as we saw in The Divine Dilemma: Part I), then He didn't need to be shamed in front of the world on the cross, He need only do it in some quiet part of nowhere. But the Word of God wanted not only to draw man away from corruption but also to teach Him and draw him to the Father by His miraculous works.

Through these works, He could persuade man that He is the Word and Wisdom of the true God, so man could again love the Father as he was made to do. St Athanasius says triumphantly: "Everything is filled with the knowledge of God." We can find God everywhere and in everything, and God the Word has encouraged us to search so that we also can do as we were made to do from the beginning.

WHAT THE SCRIPTURES SAY:

"being rooted and grounded in love, may be able to comprehend with all the saints what is the width and length and depth and height— to know the love of Christ which passes knowledge; that you may be filled with all the fullness of God." (Ephesians 3:17-19). Commenting on this, St Athanasius writes, "For the Word unfolded Himself everywhere, above and below and in the depths and in the breadth: above, in creation; below, in the incarnation; in the depths, in hell; in breadth, in the world. Everything is filled with the knowledge of God."

REFLECTION

Here we see that God had to die and resurrect openly so that all could believe in Him. Sometimes we think that our faith is only meant to be something hidden or something personal. Of course this is one aspect of our faith, where God looks to what we do in secret. However, we are also called to proclaim His death and resurrection so that people may know who He is and what He has done for us. What can we do to preach and proclaim Christ's saving act to the world?

[17]. We might be a little bit confused about how the Word of God, who made the whole world, was also able to be in the world that He made. This is the great mystery of the Incarnation. Though God's Word was in the world in a body, His wondrous work of Creation was still perceivable all around. St Athanasius says, "He was both in everything and outside all" or elsewhere "But what is most marvellous, being the Word, He was not contained by anyone, but rather Himself contained everything."

St Athanasius compares this to the way a man thinks. When someone thinks about something outside his body, he thinks about that thing but does not change it. For example, he could think about the sun but by doing that he wouldn't move the sun. But for the Word of God this wasn't the case: though He was in a body, He was able to keep all things which are outside of His body in order and to give them all life. How wondrous! What an inexplicable mystery!

[18]. If we look at the Gospels we see that Christ ate and drank. Therefore, we can see that Christ was properly present in the body, not simply as an illusion. Because of the wondrous works the Word enacted in the body, we can see that this is in fact the Son of God. We know that eating and drinking is common to all bodies, but how do we know these miracles tell us about God?

Importantly, miracles are not simply to

show off: they are revelations of who God is. St Athanasius shows that the miracles done by Jesus show that He is the Word of God.

If we think about the healing miracles that the Word did, many of those that were healed had been born without sight or without hearing or were unable to walk. Since the Word of God supplied what they didn't have from birth, we can see that He is the One who made them. His miracles reveal Him as not simply a healer but as the Creator

In a similar way, from His own birth He fashioned a body from a Virgin without a man. This reveals that He is the Maker of mankind. When He changed the water into wine, He shows Himself to be Lord and Creator of the substance of all water. When He feeds the

 REFLECTION

It is very reasonable to believe in mystery. It is a recognition that man is not able to comprehend all things in his mind, especially not things of God. For why should man expect to be able to explain all the ways of God when he fails even to explain all the ways of man? And why would man worship a God that he could completely understand? He would not be a greater being but a lesser one.

five thousand with only five loaves, He reveals Himself to be the Provider of all, the one who ensures that the crops grow and flourish, showing what He always does but this time in a miraculous way. The Word of God did not simply vaunt His power for the sake of it, but was showing us that He is God, and is God the whole time.

WHAT THE SCRIPTURES SAY:

"If I do not do the works of My Father, do not believe Me; but if I do, even if you don't believe Me, believe My works, that you might know and understand that the Father is in Me and I am in the Father." (John 10:37-38). Christ is doing the works of His Father as St Athanasius explained to us. He is revealing the Father through the wondrous works He has wrought in the body!

REFLECTION

God's miraculous works are often things that He is doing for us all the time but which are achieved in a short and miraculous way. The things He does for us are like 'little miracles' in that sense. Are we grateful for all the little miracles God does for us in our life, things we hardly ever notice like the rising sun, the nourishing rain, and the growth of the crops?

CHRISTIANITY AND THE BODY

St Athanasius makes it quite clear that the Word of God, Jesus Christ, was truly in a body – for how else could one explain that He drank and He ate? But why does he stress this so much?

There were many groups in early Christianity (and after) that tried to deny that Christ really came in a body. These particularly included the Gnostics (a Greek word meaning something like "those who know"). They were heavily influenced not only by Christianity but also by the Greek philosophers, particularly Plato. He believed that the soul was trapped inside the body. Going from this idea, the Gnostics taught that the body was evil and it was only the soul or the spirit that was good. This led them to some crazy practices. Some thought they had to destroy their body and so underwent extreme practices of starvation and mutilation. Some thought that their soul was not affected by their body and did the complete opposite! They engaged in wild drinking parties and gave in to excessive lust thinking that none of their actions could affect their soul. Even after them, the Muslims believed that Christ didn't actually die in the body and that His death was an illusion. Even more sadly, many modern Christians have fallen into the pagan trap of believing that the soul alone is good and will be saved but the body is evil.

Orthodox Christianity has been

influenced heavily by the opening chapter of the Gospel of St John, which says "And the Word became flesh and dwelt among us, and we beheld His glory, the glory as of the only begotten of the Father, full of grace and truth." (John 1:14). We believe not only in the salvation and resurrection of our souls, but in our souls and our bodies together. What does this mean? This means that we have to work with our bodies, we have to try not to destroy them with its lusts nor neglect them since they are temples for the Holy Spirit. Furthermore, we need to worship God not only with our souls but with all our minds, hearts, and strength – which means even

REFLECTION

Here we see a very important lesson. God cares about everything about us. This is because He wants us to love Him with all our heart, mind, soul, and strength. He even cares about our bodies so that we can use it for the glory of His name. Many times we neglect our body and our health, because we think that our body doesn't matter, because we're going to die anyway. But it's important to remember that while we're here on earth we are stewards of our bodies and it is up to us to take care of our bodies so that we can use it, as much as is possible, for the glory of God.

with our bodies! When we are in the liturgy we see beautiful imagery, we smell the aroma of incense, we hear divine hymns, and many of us bow down before the Lord. We worship God with our bodies.

The moral of the story is that bad theology leads to bad behaviour. We ought to reflect on the teachings of the Church so that we are not led astray by the weakness of either our body or our soul.

[19]. Therefore, we now know another reason why the Word of God appeared in the flesh, why He took on a body. By showing His good deeds and wondrous works in the body, He could help man to know God by analogy. He could redirect man from looking downwards at the world to looking upwards to God.

The demons were conquered by the Word of God and even confessed Him to be God, so man could no longer worship them instead. Even the Creation, which man had also worshipped, wasn't silent in revealing the glory of God. When the Word died on the cross, the sun turned back, the earth shook, the mountains were rent, and all were amazed. Creation shouted out that it is God's servant and that this was indeed the Son of God.

Through all these works, therefore, the God Word revealed Himself to human beings. But there is more to the Incarnation: for how can we understand it without considering the death and resurrection of the Word of God? This, St Athanasius says, is our next task.

CHAPTER II SUMMARY

What happened in this chapter is as follows:

• God had made man to be with Him all His days but man had sinned. We saw already that the Word of God had died to purify man of his corruption and to fulfil the law. But there was another reason why God needed to be incarnated: when man fell he had forgotten God and was no longer able to know Him.

• Man looked only to the world, to the demons, and to other men and made gods out of these things; he set up idols which are led to communion with death since they are away from God, and being away from God means being away from the source of life.

• In order to draw man back to the Father, the God Word took on a body and appeared in a way that man could understand. He performed many wonders and miracles so that man was able to know not only that this is God, but also to know who God truly is.

• By the divine humility of the Word of God, man could then throw away the idols and could see the true greatness of the world made by God. Everything with God becomes more wondrous and valuable than in its weakness on its own.

CHAPTER FOUR

THE DEATH OF CHRIST AND THE RESSURRECTION OF THE BODY

CHAPTER FOUR

[20]. At this point, St Athanasius recaps on what has been discovered by his inquiry so far: Whose is it to turn the corruptible to incorruptibility except the Saviour himself who made the world? Whose is it to recreate man in the image of God if not the Word of God Who is Himself the Image of God? Whose is it to raise up the mortal to immortality if not Jesus Christ, who is Life itself? And lastly, whose is it to teach about the Father and destroy the worship of idols if not the Word who is the Son of the Father and the one who arranges all things? Therefore, what must happen must indeed happen: having showed the world His works and revealed to the world His Father, the Word of God must be sacrificed on behalf of all and destroy death through His resurrection.

As a side note, St Athanasius says do not be surprised if it seems that sometimes he is repeating himself: God can be approached in many ways and in each way perhaps something else can be discovered even though it is largely the same. It is better to repeat ourselves than to fail to say or discover something important about God.

Then a great and unexplainable event occurred: the Word of God took on a corruptible body so that He may die, so that we may live. The Word of God, being immortal, could not be destroyed by death but He instead destroyed death, which had haunted man throughout his history.

What Saint Athanasius Said

"It was not for another to turn what was corruptible to incorruptibility except the Saviour Himself, who in the beginning created the universe from nothing; and... it was not for another to recreate again the 'in the image' for human beings, except the Image of the Father... it was not for another to teach about the Father... except the Word who is the true only-begotten Son of the Father."

REFLECTION

St Athanasius says that God can be approached in many ways. Therefore, there are many ways to live a Christian life. What is my way to serve God with the talents He has given me? How is it different from another person's? Do I ever try to force someone to take my path to God? Do I ever fail to share the wisdom that God has revealed to me on my path to someone on another?

[21]. Thanks to the death and resurrection, we, the "faithful in Christ", no longer suffer that law that God had set for us from the beginning [If you don't remember it, check out chapter II]. When we die, we are not lost but are like seeds sown in the ground, dissolved into the earth, that then rise up again "to attain a better resurrection" (Hebrews 11:35).

But the curious reader might think, "Now if the Word of God needed to die, why did He need to do so in front of all? Why could He not have endured a death without the shame, and instead have died in a more honourable manner?" But, St Athanasius says, if He did not die in front of all then perhaps rumours would begin. If He had died privately, people would say that He died like other men: that man, in his corrupted state, succumbs to illness and to weakness and surely the same thing has happened to Jesus the Christ. But this cannot be so because the Word of God took the body to heal it from illness and weakness, He needed to show mankind that He didn't die from these things but overcame them. It would be unfitting for the Man who healed others from their illness and weakness to fall to those same things.

But again, the inquisitive reader might ask, "Why did He not also prevent death just as He prevented illness?" But to ask this we would have to forget all that St Athanasius has said already: why did the Word of God take a body if not to die, to fulfil the law that had been set at the beginning of time, and to save man? He had to die, this was why He was incarnated. St Athanasius says also that it was unfitting that illness could even occur at all before His death lest people then assume that this was a weakness in His body. Yet again the reader might ask, "If He was free of illness, would He then not have hungered or thirsted?" Again, St Athanasius answers that yes, He would have hungered because that is a property of the body, that is part of what it means to live in a body, but that didn't lead to illness or weakness, it didn't lead to starvation, because it was the Lord who was 'wearing' this body. The holy body belonged to none other than Life itself.

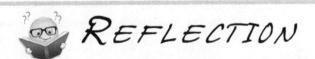

REFLECTION

With questions about our faith, we know that the house built on the sand will not stand, but that the house built on stone shall not fall. We can ask questions that can make sure that our faith (our house) is on stone and not on sand. I can ask a priest, a Sunday School servant, a parent, or a school friend. The Church provides and will always provide for its beggars.

[22]. Although St Athanasius has already patiently answered many questions, like a loving father, he continues to answer more. Why did Christ not hide from the council of the Jews and preserve His body as immortal? He explains that this was unsuitable for the Lord. We have already seen that He had to die, and it is not fitting that He should do it Himself, for how could God, who is Life, cause His own death? So, He must accept it from others, without making them do so, so that He could destroy it.

We need to remember here that He is not coming to die His own death, He is not revealing any weakness on His part here in succumbing to death. On the contrary, He has come in strength to die not His own death but the death of mankind. The Word of God, being Life, has no death of His own but took the death of humankind instead that He might destroy it. Just as one receives a trophy for hard work, so has Christ received the resurrection for His conquering of death.

Again, St Athanasius emphasises that there was no way the Word could have succumbed to illness. How could He have been able to heal others of illness if His own body, His own temple, was defiled with illness? People again would say that either He does not have the power or that He has the power but refuses to use it because He lacks love for humanity. Surely this is not the case!

[23]. St Athanasius sees that many people struggle with the idea that God died. People, rightly so, struggle with the thought that the mighty God Who created all that can be seen, somehow not only took on a body but actually died in that body. He continues asking questions in order to convince people that not only did it happen, it simply had to happen.

Suppose that the Word had gone and hidden Himself in some secret part of the world in order to perform His death and His resurrection. Suppose after having done that, He came back to everyone – His disciples, the Jews, and the Gentiles – and declared to them that He had died and risen from the dead. What would they think? Surely they would claim that He is telling tales. Death must occur before resurrection, St Athanasius says. Therefore, if the death is unseen and unwitnessed occurring in a secret place before no one, so too will the resurrection be unseen and unwitnessed.

Furthermore, why would He proclaim His resurrection if He did not reveal His death? Why would He have performed all those wondrous acts and miracles in front of many if not to reveal Himself as the Word of God? How could His disciples preach the resurrection at all if they were not convinced that He had truly died? How could the Word of God have revealed his victory over death if He had performed it all in secret and in silent? This could certainly not be the case. It is completely inconsistent with all His actions beforehand and with the very purpose of His coming to earth.

REFLECTION

St Athanasius said that the Disciples would not have been able to preach had they not witnessed the resurrection and had the faith that they had. We need first of all to work on our own faith in order to be a faithful witness of God to others. We need to remember Christ's words: "Hypocrite! First remove the plank from your own eye, and then you will see clearly to remove the speck from your brother's eye." (Matthew 7:5).

[24]. So, the Word of God certainly needed to die, and He needed to die in front of people and not in secret. But why did He have to die in such a horrific way? Couldn't the Word have devised a death for Himself that was more glorious and 'worthy' of Him? St Athanasius responds to this question with another analogy: consider a noble wrestler (wrestling was real back then). When he goes to fight, he doesn't choose his opponent himself, in case people start to think he is choosing someone weak or that he is afraid of another. Instead, he allows the crowd to choose his opponent so that he can show that he is superior to their best and therefore to all. In the same way, the Word of God allowed the crowd to determine the method of His death. He did not choose, lest someone suspect He was fearful of a particular method of death, but He let the wicked crowd devise their most treacherous scheme and vile method of slaying Him, of killing Life itself, so that He could show them all that He is truly the Word of the Father.

Here something wondrous happened: "that dishonourable death which they thought to inflict, this was the trophy of his victory over death." Furthermore, unlike the beheading of John or the sawing apart of Isaiah the prophet, when Christ was slain His body was undivided and whole. Now, His body is the Church itself which also ought to be undivided and whole. But man, in his wickedness, ever strives against Him.

[25]. Previously, St Athanasius has been answering questions from non-believers particularly (but also believers to some extent). He has been giving 'logical' answers. But if there are some noble Christians asking questions not to try to embarrass Christianity but for love of learning, St Athanasius offers a 'theological' answer as to why the Word of God had to die on the cross.

Firstly, He had to die in order to "become a curse" (Galatians 3:13) for us, or to take up and destroy our curse which is death. More specifically, that curse is not just death but death on a cross for it says in Deuteronomy 21:23, "Cursed is he who hangs from the tree."

REFLECTION

That wrestling analogy should really leave an impression on us! How comforting is it to know that our God can face anything thrown at Him? It should fill us with such confidence that whatever I'm facing in my life – whether it's difficulties at school, or with my friends, or with my health – no matter what it is, I have an all-powerful, all-conquering God who has my back!

Secondly, only in dying on the cross does Christ die with arms open and His hands stretched in either direction. St Athanasius says that when He died as a ransom for all, He destroyed the "wall of partition" (Ephesians 2:14), the wall that separates the Gentiles from the Jews. Thus, looking upon the Word of God on the cross with His hands outstretched, He draws in the Gentiles with one hand and the Jews with the other that they may unite in His body. And we know, of course, that His body is nothing but the Church! What a beautiful image and wise explanation of such a vile death!

Thirdly, in dying on the cross, the Word of God was raised up in the air. This was said to be the domain of Satan, the Prince of lies, whom St Paul describes as "The prince of power of the air, who is now at work in the sons of disobedience" (Ephesians 2:2). Rising up to the air on the cross, Christ overthrew the devil and purified the air. Only by cleansing the air could He declare, "I saw Satan falling as lightning" (Luke 10:18). Furthermore, He prophesied He would do this in John 12:32 "When I am lifted up, I shall draw all to Myself." Having sanctified the air of the wickedness of the devil, He blazed the trail for us to follow Him into heaven, as was written by the psalmist "Lift up your gates, O princes of yours, and be raised up, everlasting gates!" (Psalms 24:7).

It is for these theological reasons, which are logical in their own way, that the Word of

God had to be lifted up on a cross, purify the air, draw all people into His body, and lead man into heaven.

WHAT THE SCRIPTURES SAY:

Notice how well St Athanasius knows the Scriptures! He does something that all the Fathers do: interprets the Bible 'Christologically'. This is a fancy word coming from 'Christology', the theology and understanding of who Christ is (Christ calls upon us to answer this in Mark 8:27: "Who do people say that I am?"). To interpret the Scriptures Christologically means to find Christ on every page and in every verse of the Bible. It means that there is a deeper and more wondrous meaning than just the literal. If we can interpret the Scriptures firstly Christologically, then by God's grace and guidance we may be able to interpret and view the world Christologically.

REFLECTION

See how here Christ took something that had become evil and made it good! In dying on the cross, and dying in the world, He saved more than just mankind but the whole world for He came "for the life of the world" (John 6:51).

Now everything is more wonderful because it has been saved by Christ. This is a mystery that we cannot perfectly understand, but we can look at the world in wonder. For God made the world out of His love, and He saved it out of His love. Everywhere and in everything is love.

[26]. We have seen now that the Word of God had to die by the cross, that it made both logical and theological sense. But now we can ask, why did He spend three days before He was resurrected? What was the meaning of that? St Athanasius says that it was neither too long nor too short, but just right.

Suppose that the Word of God had been raised up immediately, that on the same day as when He died He had also arisen. What will the world assume? Surely, they will say, this Man never died at all! If He had not died, then the glory of incorruptibility would have been obscured, and His victory over death would be unclear. No, He couldn't be raised up as early as that.

Suppose instead that He had remained even longer in the tomb than three days, and that He had made sure that people knew that He was well and truly dead before resurrecting. Yet, surely people would disbelieve that it was Him at all, or that this was truly the same body that had died. They would think that this is a different body, or even a different person! Certainly, that's not acceptable.

But instead, on the third day, while the disciples were in mourning and the peoples were confused because they thought that their hopes had been shattered, on the third day, when the word 'Jesus' was still on the lips of the gossiping townsfolk and the word 'Christ' was still in their minds, on that day

What Saint Athanasius Said

"But while the word was still echoing in their ears and their eyes were still expecting and their minds were in suspense, and those who put him to death and witnessed the death of the lordly body were still living upon earth and in the same place, the Son of God Himself, after an interval of three days, showed the body which had been dead as immortal and incorruptible; and it was demonstrated to all that the body died not by the weakness of the nature of the indwelling Word, but in order that death might be destroyed in it through the power of the Saviour."

He was raised up. On that day He revealed the same body, the same man, truly having died and truly having come to life that all may believe! On that day, He showed His victory over death to all and for all.

[27]. Christ, the Word of God, has truly conquered and triumphed over death. Death itself has died. So, what does this mean? Can we see any difference in the world? Surely, St Athanasius says, it is quite clear. Since the Saviour has raised His body from the dead, death is no longer feared but trampled on and mocked by believers. Indeed, they – the true believers and followers in Christ – would rather choose the path of death than deny their faith, which is in a way an even worse death, a separation from Life who is God.

Look at mankind before Christ. They trembled at death and wept profusely at the passing of those dear to them. Death was truly the last enemy to be destroyed (1 Corinthians 15:26). Yet now, when man has come to faith, they "so despise death that they eagerly rush to it and become witnesses to the resurrection over it effected by the Saviour." For proof of the resurrection, St Athanasius simply says:

History of the Church:

When St Athanasius was writing, there had been many persecutions of the Church, most recently the Decian Persecution that ended near the start of the 4th Century. It was said by Tertullian (an early Christian that sadly went mad in his later life) that if the martyrs of the world were put on a scale, it would be balanced by the martyrs of Egypt. To be a Christian then was a matter of life or death quite literally. Today, it is still a matter of life or death, but we fail to see it clearly for it is instead Christ's Life or absence of Him which is death. When we look at our faith in terms of life or death, perhaps we can then take it a little more seriously.

look at the martyrs. Though mankind was paralysed in fear of death, now it is as if it is nothing. Where does this powerful faith and valiant bravery come from if not from Christ's victory over death in His resurrection?

St Athanasius uses another of his famous analogies and describes death as such: imagine a tyrant, a cruel king, that has stolen the throne and was now slayed by the legitimate king. This king has bound the tyrant by hand and foot, the king's subjects mock him, hit him, and revile him, and no longer fear the one whose fury and barbarity was a cause for so much of their suffering because the legitimate and victorious king has come. In this way, the cross and Christ's resurrection have overthrown the tyrant death and we may say with St Paul, "Death, where is thy victory? Hades, where is thy sting?" (1 Corinthians 15:55).

REFLECTION

St Athanasius uses Christians as evidence for his argument that Christ was truly raised from the dead – as our belief in Him is proof of the eye-witnessing of the Apostles, which they then passed on. We are all therefore on display for the world, and we are all called to be witnesses to Christ. Our failing can lead to the failing of others. How much more, then, do we need to live truly faithful and Christian lives? We must realise that the whole world depends on it!

[28]. Surely this is a strong argument for the death and resurrection of our Lord, says St Athanasius. Adding to it, he reminds us that it is in fact man's nature to fear death and the decomposition of the body. And yet, by Christ's victory over death man is able to transcend, to go beyond, his very nature!

Consider this: we know that it is the nature of fire to burn things. Suppose someone said that there was some material that is not afraid of burning but rather shows fire to be weak (the Indians at the time of St Athanasius correctly said this about asbestos), then all you need to do is to test it out: cover your hands in asbestos and put it in the fire to see if it is true, to see if it burns. (Please don't try this at home; the Indians probably didn't know that asbestos is terrible for your lungs). Similarly, if someone wanted to see that the tyrant (mentioned in the last chapter) was truly overthrown and bound, one need only enter his domain and see for oneself.

So, if someone disbelieves St Athanasius' arguments, he need only look at the martyrs and see that if the argument of the mind is unclear, surely the argument of the heart and of the body is obvious. Surely one can see the martyrs trampling on death. But if this is not enough, if somehow what is obvious and clear before your eyes is not enough then come, put on Christ yourself, and see the power of faith in Him. Accept His death and resurrection, accept faith in Him, accept His teaching, and the power of death will disappear from you and His victory over it will be made clear. St Athanasius here simply says, "Come and see" (John 1:39).

[29]. Now we have been given resounding evidence for the Word of God's sojourn on earth, His incarnation, His dying, and His rising, but we have also been given evidence for the works of His followers in trampling on death as He first did. Indeed, according to St Athanasius there is now no good reason to deny any of this at all.

He tells us to think of things like this: imagine it is night time and there is darkness. As night ends steadily the sun appears and every earthly place is enlightened by its rays. There is no doubt, then that the sun has caused this brightness and that it has chased away and banished the darkness. So it is with death being despised and trampled on. And this all occurred after what momentous event? What else but the resurrection of Christ!

Furthermore, when you see a snake trampled upon and lifeless you know that it is certainly dead because you are aware of its usual aggressiveness and ferocity. Similarly, when you see a lion being played with by children, you know that it is either dead or has lost all its power. Just as it is clear for the eye to see these things, so too is it clear that when death is despised by disciples of Christ that death too is dead, destroyed, and trampled upon! No doubt remains! There is no reason for unbelief! Death is gone, and corruption is made into incorruption!

[30]. By arguments and also through facts and events it has been shown that Christ trampled on death and came back to life, and following on from this what else will happen other than that the body should rise if death has been put to death itself? But yet, there is more to say! There is more evidence that Christ is alive to this day!

Firstly, we have to say that it is clear that if anyone is dead, that person cannot act: "deeds and actions towards other human beings only belong to the living." But if we also look around us what do we see? We see the Saviour working to bring many people from around the world to Him, and we see people rejecting the teaching of their fathers to turn to Christ. Is this the action of one who is dead?

Furthermore, if He is dead and not acting, then how does the adulterer stop in His name, how does the murderer no longer murder, the thief no longer steal, the blasphemer no longer blaspheme? By whose power are these accomplished? How are demons cast out in His name, and idols shown to be worthless through the same? St Athanasius says, "This is not the work of one dead, but of one alive, and especially of God." Now, it is simply absurd for anyone to believe that Christ simply died and that nothing more happened after it.

[31]. Having seen the wondrous things that Christ has accomplished and continues to accomplish, showing Him to be truly alive,

what can we make of idols and false gods? Surely it is clear that they are destroyed, abandoned, and have well and truly ceased. It is not they who cast out Christ, but Christ who casts them out. Meanwhile the Son of God is "living and active" (Hebrews 4:12).

The one who disbelieves the resurrection of the body of the Lord, is likely ignorant of the power of the Word and of the Wisdom of God. These people who deny the resurrection are probably ignorant of all that has gone on before, and of all that has been shown and discussed earlier. They are unaware that the Word had to take a body. Of course, He took a body like ours, that is, a mortal body. Therefore, He had to die as due to this mortality, and since this was why He came. Yet this body could not remain dead, for it is the temple of Life itself. This body died as a mortal, but rose up because of the life that was in it: Life itself, Jesus Christ the Word of the Father.

 ## REFLECTION

"For it is true that the dead can effect nothing, but the Saviour effects such great things every day – drawing to piety, persuading to virtue, teaching about immortality, leading to a desire for heavenly things, revealing the knowledge of the Father, inspiring power against death, showing Himself to each, and purging away the godlessness of idols."

[32]. What of those people who refuse the resurrection because they have not seen it themselves? What should we say to them? First, we need to declare that since God is unseen – we are not able to see Him as if He were hiding in the sky – but we know Him by His works. If there were no works, perhaps one could disbelieve Him, but if there are works then one would be mad to deny Him and His resurrection.

Though many fail to believe, if they look instead to the deeds accomplished by those who believe they will see the power of Christ. How would demons be cast out in Christ's name if He were dead? Surely the demons would not obey a dead man. Yet they see the unseen and cry out "We know who You are: the Holy One of God" (Luke 4:34) and elsewhere again, "Ah, what have we to do with You, Son of God? I beseech You, do not torment me" (Matthew 8:28; Mark 5:7). Just as death offered the tool by which the Word of God was victorious, so do the demons offer the evidence that reveal Him as Son of God.

Now let no one deny it, Jesus Christ is truly the Father's Word, Wisdom, and Power. He took up a body for the salvation of all, He revealed the Father to us, destroyed death, gave incorruptibility to all through the resurrection, and raised His body as the first-fruits and as a sign of the victory over death. And all this through the cross. Come, now, let us glorify Him!

CHAPTER IV SUMMARY

What happened in this chapter is as follows:

- St Athanasius explained why Christ had to die and why He had to die in the manner that He did. He asked why in front of all these people (chapter 21 & 23), why He couldn't choose a 'worthy' way to die (chapter 24), why it had to be on a cross (chapter 25), and why He stayed in the tomb for three days (chapter 26), among other questions

- That Christ has died and has come back from the dead is made known to all by the actions of His followers: no longer is death feared

- That Christ is still alive is shown by the power He still has in the world: the demons are cast out in His name and His followers get strength and crush evil by His name

- St Athanasius concludes that if one has followed everything that he has shown so far, it is absurd not to believe

CHAPTER FIVE

REFUTATION OF THE JEWS

CHAPTER FIVE

[33]. Now remember that this whole book was written by St Athanasius as a letter to his friend Makarios to convince him of and strengthen him in the Christian doctrine. Part of that job is to show him why some of the detractors of Christianity aren't correct. The detractors he takes on are the same as St Paul took on in Corinthians: the Jews who declare Christ as a stumbling block and the Greeks who declare Him as foolishness, yet we know He is the Power and Wisdom of God (1 Corinthians 1:23-24).

In this chapter St Athanasius plans to refute the Jews first, and in order to do this he bases it on his common ground with them: the Scriptures, and specifically the Old Testament. Over the whole chapter, St Athanasius shows his knowledge of the Scriptures and, most importantly, that he finds Christ in all of it.

He starts with Isaiah 7:14, "Behold a virgin will conceive and bear a son, and they will call his name Emmanuel, which is interpreted as 'God with us.'" Clearly, there is a prophecy of a virgin birth and that this virgin gives birth to the Saviour! Now with this Saviour, what do the Scriptures say about Him? Moses tells us that "A star will rise from Jacob and a human being from Israel, and he will break down the princes of Moab." (Numbers 24:17). So from this (as well as Numbers 24:5-7 and Isaiah 8:4), we see that this same Saviour, the Messiah, will be a human being. But not just a human being, for Isaiah again says "Behold, the Lord sits upon a swift cloud, and he will come to Egypt, and the graven images of Egypt shall be shaken" (Isaiah 19:1). So, it is the Lord who will be the Saviour that comes to Egypt. But not simply that, for Hosea writes "From Egypt have I called my Son" (Hosea 11:1).

What has St Athanasius shown so far from the Old Testament? He says that the Saviour will be born of a virgin, He will be called 'Emmanuel', will be a human being, is also the Lord, but last of all is the Son of God. Sound like anyone familiar? Surely this is no other than Jesus Christ, the Saviour who is born of the virgin St Mary, is man and God, is the Son of God, and who was in our midst as Emmanuel.

 REFLECTION

St Athanasius starts his discussion with the Jews by finding common ground with them. Often in our day-to-day dealings with people it is more important for us to focus on our common ground than on our differences. By doing this, we can debate with people with our hearts which is far more powerful than just debating with our heads. We should always remember when we are discussing things with people, that our aim is not to win the argument, but rather our aim is to win the person.

[34]. The Scriptures have thus revealed the Saviour to us. But from above He sounds like a warrior or a king on the earth, and not quite as the crucified Christ. Yet St Athanasius shows that Scriptures are certainly not silent about His death, we need only look again to Isaiah, particularly chapter 53:3-10.

"He bears our sins and suffers for our sake; we considered Him to be in distress and affliction, and suffering. He was wounded for our sins and bruised for our iniquities. The chastisement of our peace is upon Him, by His bruise we have been healed" (Isaiah 53:4-5). This man who saved us suffered for us. St Athanasius says that "He is dishonoured for our sake that we might be honoured."

And why did He come? Isaiah is not silent on this either saying "For all we like sheep have gone astray; the human being has gone astray from his way, and the Lord has delivered Him to our sins." (Isaiah 53:6). He came to redeem man from sins that had turned him away from God, as St Athanasius explained in Chapter II and III.

Now, before anyone claims that this was only a human read on: "For He committed no iniquity, nor was deceit found in His mouth. And the Lord wishes to Heal him from His iniquity." (Isaiah 53:9-10). No human being has committed no iniquity, nor has had no deceit – in other words, no one has never sinned. Except for Christ who "was in all points tempted as we are, yet without sin"

(Hebrews 4:15). This is an uncanny prophecy from the 8th century BC, 800 years before Christ!

WHAT THE SCRIPTURES SAY:

Read the whole prophecy in Isaiah 53:3-10 as it appears in the text from St Athanasius "A man in affliction and knowing how to bear sorrows, because his face was turned away. He was despised and esteemed not. He bears our sins and suffers for our sake; we considered him to be in distress and affliction, and suffering. He was wounded for our sins and bruised for our iniquities. The chastisement of our peace is upon him, by his bruise we have been healed. For all we like sheep have gone astray; the human being has gone astray from his way, and the Lord has delivered him to our sins. And he, though being in affliction, opens not his mouth. Like a sheep led to the slaughter, and as a lamb before its shearers is dumb, so opens he not his mouth. In his humiliation his judgement was taken away. Who will declare his generation? For his life was taken from the earth. By the iniquities of the people he was brought to death. And I shall give the wicked in exchange for his burial and the rich for his death, for he committed no iniquity, nor was deceit found in his mouth. And the Lord wishes to heal him from his iniquity."

[35]. The death of the Messiah was declared in Scriptures and, St Athanasius says, even the manner of his death is evident in Scriptures. It is clear in the Old Testament

"Was not Abel from Adam, Enoch from Yared, Noah from Lamech, Abraham from Tarrah, Isaac from Abraham, and Jacob from Isaac? Was not Judah from Jacob, and Moses and Aaron from Ameram? Was not Samuel from Helcana, David from Jesse, Solomon from David, Hezekiah from Achaz, Josiah from Amos, Isaiah from Amos, Jeremiah from Hilciah, Ezekiel from Buzi? Did not each of these have his father as the author of his being? Who then is born of a virgin only?

that the Messiah will die on a cross. Firstly, he quotes Moses who writes "You will see your life hanging before your eyes, and you will not believe" (Deuteronomy 28:66) – remember that God is Life itself, since He made us out of nothing and we depend on Him completely for existence. So it seems that God is hanging before their eyes. St Athanasius then quotes Psalm 21:17-19, "They pierced my hands and my feet; they numbered all my bones, they divided my garments among them, and for my vesture they cast lots." But what death takes place hanging in the air, where hands and feet are pierced, except the death of the Cross?

These aren't the only things that reveal Christ as the Messiah. The whole of Scripture is a testament to Him. Look at the Patriarchs of the Scriptures, which of them in the whole of the Old Testament was born without a father? Which woman in the Old Testament was able to bring forth a child without a man? When Moses was born, he was hidden by his parents; and not even David's neighbours knew of him since the great Samuel had to ask Jesse if he had another son. But Christ's birth was testified with a star in heaven, from which he descended.

[36]. "Before the child knows how to cry out 'father' or 'mother.' He will take the power of Damascus and the spoils of Samaria before the King of Assyria" (Isaiah 8:4). St Athanasius takes this prophecy and asks about all the patriarchs who have gone

before: which of them have fulfilled it? Wasn't David thirty years old before he began to reign, and Solomon a young man? Didn't Joas and Josiah become kings when they were seven years old? Surely all of these could cry out 'father' or 'mother.'

Who, apart from Christ, was reigning and despoiling his enemies almost before his birth? And which king of Israel was it that "in him will the nations hope" (Isaiah 11:10). Was there ever a king while Jerusalem stood in whom all the nations put their hope? There was never peace for the Israelites in Jerusalem! None of these fulfilled the prophecies. Which of these died on the cross for the salvation of all? Which of these went down to Egypt and destroyed the idols? Abraham and Moses went to Egypt, yet idolatry remained universal. Surely it was none of these that fulfilled the prophecies.

[37]. St Athanasius goes on searching for anyone who could pass as the Messiah in the Old Testament, asking who died on the cross for the salvation of all? He writes, "Abraham died, expiring on a bed; Isaac and Jacob also died with feet raised upon a bed. Moses and Aaron on the mountain; David died in his house, without being the object of any plotting by the people... Isaiah was sawn asunder, but he was not hanged upon the wood; Jeremiah was abused, but he did not die under condemnation; Ezekiel suffered, but not for the people, but indicating what would happen to the people." Furthermore, all of these were merely human beings. But the

> ### What Saint Athanasius Said
>
> *"He it is that was crucified, with the sun and creation as witnesses together with those who inflicted death upon Him; and by His death salvation has come to all, and all creation has been ransomed. He it is Who is the Life of all, and Who like a sheep, delivered His own body to death as a substitute for the salvation of all, even if the Jews do not believe."*

Scriptures say, "You will see your life hanging before your eyes" (Deuteronomy 28:66) so it must be more than just a man. And "Who will declare his generation?" (Isaiah 53:8), who knows His father, since generations were known in history through the father (e.g. Abraham begot Isaac, Isaac begot Jacob etc.).

So, who do the Scriptures speak about and the Prophets declare? There is none other but Jesus Christ. He is the only One who died on the cross for the salvation of all. He is the only One Who was born of a virgin and Whose generation in the flesh none can speak of for it is a mystery. He is the only One that fulfils Scripture and about Whom Scripture cries out. He is the One Who made the star declare His birth in a body, for as He came down from heaven it was necessary to have a sign in the heavens; as He is the King of creation, it was necessary that He be known by the inhabited

REFLECTION

it is said again and again that Jesus is the "King of creation." We, in His image, are the stewards or the priests of creation. We need to love one another but also love the creation that God has given us, for "God saw everything that He had made, and indeed it was very good." (Gen 1:31).

world. Jesus Christ is the One! The only one.

[38]. If all these proofs are insufficient, then there are yet still more. St Athanasius draws our attention again to Isaiah: "I was made manifest to them that sought me not; I was found by those who did not ask for me. I said, 'Here am I' to the Gentiles who did not call upon my name. I stretched out my hands to a disobedient and rebellious people" (Isaiah 65:1-2). Now who is the subject of this? If it is the prophet, then how do we explain that he became 'manifest' if he was never hidden? And when did he stretch out his hands? But if we look instead to the Word of God who was without a body, He became manifest in a body in these recent times. Again, He stretched His hands out on the cross to draw in all nations.

If this again is not sufficient what of this passage: "Be strong, weak hands and feeble knees; be consoled, faint-hearted in spirit; be

REFLECTION

St Athanasius gives very many arguments and just when you think the issue is solved he offers another one! His arguments are to convince the mind but often it's not the mind that needs convincing but the heart, for the peoples' hearts are hardened against God. The only way to undo a hardened heart is to melt it with love. While arguments are important (for Christ is Logos, He is Word and Reason) even more important is that love is shown.

strong, fear not, for behold our God requites judgement; He will come and save us. Then will the eyes of the blind be opened, and the ears of the deaf will hear; then will the lame leap like a deer and the tongue of those who stammer will be clear" (Isaiah 35:3-6). Does this not declare the coming of God and the signs that will declare Him? But when did these things happen in the history of Israel? Yes, Naaman the leper was cleansed, and Elijah and Elisha raised the dead, but no deaf person heard, nor did a blind one from birth regain his sight, nor did the lame walk. Since these things are so important and could declare the arrival of the Messiah, surely if they had occurred someone would have included them in Scriptures! Yet there is only one place where we find these things: the Gospels! It is Christ alone that fulfils this prophecy. "From the ages never has it been heard that anyone opened the eyes of a man born blind. If this man were not from God, He could do nothing" (John 9:32-33).

[39]. What if someone were to say: "This is all well and good if you are looking for a Messiah in the past, in the Scriptures, but what if you are still awaiting the Messiah? Could He not still be coming?" Yet St Athanasius says the Scriptures have an answer to even this. He quotes Daniel, the wisest man who lived, saying "Seventy weeks are decreed for your people, and your holy city, to put an end to sin, and to seal up sins, and to efface iniquities, and to atone for iniquities, and to

bring in everlasting righteousness, and to seal both vision and prophet, and to anoint the holy of holies; and that you might know and understand from the going forth of the Word to give an answer and to build Jerusalem until Christ be prince" (Daniel 9:24-25).

How does this prove that Christ had to be the Messiah? Firstly, it is clearly speaking about a Messiah for it writes of the 'holy of holies', rather than just holy men. It also says that this 'holy of holies' has to be anointed – the Greek word for the anointed one is 'Christ.'

Later it says, "to build Jerusalem until Christ be prince", in other words that Jerusalem must stand until Christ be prince. And it did, the destruction of the Temple, the epicentre of Jerusalem, (prophesied by Christ Himself) occurred ~40 years after His death (~70 AD). The Messiah had to have come before this point, and who else is there but Christ? It also says that the people have 'to seal both vision and prophet', or in other words that the prophecies and visions must end. And surely, they had ended by Christ's time, where there is no further prophecy of the Scriptures. Who else could this refer to but Jesus Christ, the Word of the Father?

[40]. No argument remains to them: it is clear that Jesus is the Messiah. The prophets no longer arise, visions are no longer given, and Jerusalem had fallen. As St Athanasius says, "For when He Who was indicated has

come, what is the use of those who indicate? When the truth is present, what need is there any more for the shadow?"

St Athanasius is not alone in saying this, as Moses says the same "There will not be lacking a prince from Judah or a leader from his loins, until what is laid up for him comes, and he is the expectation of the nations" (Gen 49:10). He declares that the Lord will never depart from His people until fullness comes, until the Christ comes. Having been declared by Moses, this is known and declared by no one less than Christ Himself: "The Law and prophets prophesied until John (Matthew 11:13).

What's the conclusion? St Athanasius says: "But if there is neither king nor vision, but all prophecy has henceforth been sealed up, and the city and the temple taken, why are they so impious and perverse, that they see what has happened, and yet deny Christ Who made these things happen?"

Finally, the Gentiles have turned to the God of Abraham, Isaac, and Jacob, but the Jews have denied Him. They deny the One Who has illumined the inhabited world as the Scriptures say: "The Lord God has appeared to us" (Psalm 117:27), and "He sent His Word and healed them" (Psalm 106:20), and "Not a messenger, nor an angel, but the Lord Himself has saved them" (Isaiah 11:9).

What more is there for God to do to reveal Himself and declare that the Christ has come? He says it best himself: "For what more has He Who is expected by them to do when He comes? Call the Gentiles? But they have already been called. To make prophet and king and vision to cease? This has already happened. To refute the godlessness of idols? It has already been refuted and condemned. To destroy death? It is already destroyed. What then must Christ do, which has not been done? Or what is left unfulfilled, that the Jews now rejoice and disbelieve. For if, as we thus see, they have neither king, nor prophet, nor Jerusalem, nor sacrifice, nor vision, but the whole world is filled with the knowledge of God, and those from the Gentiles are abandoning godlessness, and henceforth taking refuge in the God of Abraham through the Word, our Lord Jesus Christ, it should be clear to those who are exceedingly obstinate

REFLECTION

It is easy for us to judge the Jews and wonder, how can they not believe when there is so much evidence in front of them. But instead of judging them, it's important we look at ourselves and ask are we sometimes blinded to God's hand in our lives, and to the proof of His existence? Do we forget the blessings in our lives, and the simple things he does for us day-by-day?

that Christ has come, and that He illumines absolutely all with His light and teaches the true and divine teaching concerning His Father."

CHAPTER V SUMMARY

What happened in this chapter is as follows:

• St Athanasius declares that by using the Scriptures themselves, and the Scriptures which Christians and Jew share, he can show that Christ is the Saviour

• Firstly, Scriptures declare the birth from a Virgin (Isaiah 7:14), that the one who comes is man (Numbers 24:5-7;17), God (Isaiah 19:1), and the Son of God (Hosea 11:1)

• Secondly, the Scriptures describe the way the Messiah would die (Isaiah 53:3-10; Psalms 21:17-19; Deuteronomy 28:66)

• Thirdly, that no Patriarch in the Scriptures beforehand has fulfilled the Old Testament prophecies for the Messiah

• Fourthly and finally, that the prophets have ceased, the visions have stopped, Jerusalem and the temple have fallen and that the Christ had to have come before the last of these: the only one who could have fulfilled these prophecies is Christ and thus, if you believe in the Scriptures you must also believe in Jesus Christ, the Word of the Father, Who fulfils them.

Chapter Six

CHAPTER SIX

REFUTATION OF THE GENTILES

[41]. In this chapter, St Athanasius now turns to deal with the arguments of the Greeks. Remember that his arguments are directed towards a Greek pagan mind and so to the Greeks, he became like a Greek (cf. 1 Corinthians 9:20-22). One of their main disagreements with Christianity is the idea that God appeared in a body. Many will believe in a 'Word of God', or God's wisdom, and declare that this being is the creator of the world, the ruler of creation, and the one through whom the universe is enlightened and receives its being. [The Greeks often called this creator the 'demiurge', different to the Word of God but similar enough for St Athanasius' argument]. They also believe that the cosmos is a 'body' (like a 'body' of water), it is physical and it is subject to our senses. So, it seems they already believe that the Word of God has a body – for He is the maker of the cosmos and present in it and the cosmos itself is a body!

It is then not absurd at all that this same Word of God should have a human body if He is part of the Cosmos which is itself a body. St Athanasius writes, "For the human race is part of the whole; and if the part is unsuitable to be His instrument towards the knowledge of His divinity, it would be most absurd that He should be made known even through the whole cosmos." How can He appear in the cosmos if He's unwilling to appear in part of it?

[42]. St Athanasius dwells on this point further. Being present in the whole it is not absurd to be present in a part, it is like a man's strength which is present in his whole body but can be made manifest in the foot (e.g. if he tramples on something). If Christ is everywhere present, surely it can't be denied that He is present in each part, surely it can't be denied that He can be in a single body and make up the whole body of the cosmos.

So, it seems that the Word of God is in the whole body and manifests Himself in its parts. Does He ever reveal Himself in other parts instead of the body He was incarnate in? Certainly! No one would consider it unreasonable that He appears in the sun or moon or heaven or earth or waters or fire (these things the Greeks would have agreed to, since they sacrificed to gods to calm the elements). The Lord sends rain on the just and on the unjust (Matthew 5:45), thus He acts in other parts of the world and of the body of the cosmos. In this way, St Athanasius writes beautifully, He "invisibly shows Himself" and reveals the Father.

St Athanasius gives another beautiful example: think of the mind (or the soul), it fills the whole human body, yet its thoughts can be revealed by the tongue alone and no one would say that the mind has lessened its powers in doing so. Let no one say that it is improper for the Word of God, being present in the whole, to be present in a part.

[43]. If we accept that it's reasonable that the Word of God came into a body, why did He have to come into a human body? Couldn't He have appeared in something more noble or something more majestic? But we are forgetting that He didn't come simply to dazzle His beholders, but to heal and to teach those who were suffering. And who were those suffering if not the humans?

Remember that it was man alone, with his gift of free will, who turned away from God and began to fabricate false gods out of demons and humans. All the rest of creation had not disobeyed God, but instead continued to be what they were made to be. Then it only made sense to be incarnate as a human rather than anything else because the goodness of God compelled Him! This way He could heal fallen humanity and reveal to them God the Father. This way, "since human beings were

REFLECTION

"Now nothing in creation had gone astray in its notions of God, save the human being only. Why, neither sun nor moon nor heaven nor stars nor water nor air altered their course; but knowing their Creator and King, the Word, they remained as they were made."

not able to know Him in the whole, they should not fail to know Him in the part." This way man could learn from a human body, which was far easier to understand than a cosmic body.

[44]. But there are more questions. Couldn't God, who is all powerful, simply save mankind by a nod if He wished it? Couldn't He have solved this whole dilemma in this way, just as He made mankind, and spare His Word from having to take up a body at all? What a tough question!

Yet, St Athanasius says that there are two things that need to be known to understand why this simply could not be so. Firstly, this would have worked a treat had human beings not been created already. But that's exactly the problem: they had already been created, had already become corrupted and hence needed to be healed. How could He heal them in this way without destroying them completely? If it was non-existent things that needed salvation, this nod would have been all well and good, but for existent things that are ailing and spiraling towards peril, this simply wouldn't work.

Secondly, the corruption that had occurred to man was inside the body, not outside the body. In order to confront death and destroy it, the Word of God had to put on a body to meet His foe. Had it been outside, He could simply have nodded and destroyed it. But corruption and death had taken hold of the body, so Life Itself, the Word of God, had to enter into the same to destroy death. What's more, how could any know that He is Life if He didn't make that which was mortal immortal?

St Athanasius gives us an analogy to understand: suppose you have straw. Straw is naturally destroyed by fire and if you keep it away from the fire it won't burn, but it will still be afraid of the fire for the fire still has power over it. But if you cover the straw with asbestos, which is fireproof, then the straw will not burn, and it will no longer fear the fire but trample on it. The body is the same: if death were kept from it by command, it would still fear death and be servant to it. But if it has been freed of its corruption, it fears death no longer. Indeed, it tramples on death.

[45]. There is little more for St Athanasius to say on that topic, it seems clear that God the Word took on human flesh to give life to the body and to reveal Himself to and be known by His creation. Now, that prophecy of Isaiah

 REFLECTION

The Lord could have chosen to destroy mankind for our disobedience and solve His dilemma, but instead He chose to reveal Himself to us and suffer on the cross for us. Are we willing to suffer in innocence for Him or for others just as He suffered in innocence for us?

has been fulfilled: "The whole earth was filled with the knowledge of the Lord" (Isaiah 11:9). Now everywhere man looks, he cannot help but see God. If he looks up to the heaven, he sees its orderly arrangement and is reminded of its orderly arranger. If he looks at humans, he sees the image in which they were made (God's image). If he looks and is turned astray by demons, he sees demons being cast out by the Word of God and judges that He is their master. If He looks down to the heroes in Hades, he is reminded of the one whom death could not contain and who resurrected on the third day. St Athanasius writes, "The Lord touched all parts of creation and freed and disabused everything from error."

[46]. What other evidence do we have against the Greeks, asks St Athanasius? We need only see the state of their own religion. Humans have abandoned the worship of the Greek idols and deities and their oracles have stopped. Those heroes that the poets praised are being mocked as simply mere humans. Demons and the deceptive craft of magic is being trampled underfoot. All in all, the wisdom of the Greeks has become foolish (cf. 1 Corinthians 1:18-24). And when did all this happen? Only after Jesus Christ, the Word of the Father, took a body as a temple and dwelt in it.

What's more, He has transcended space as well. In the past, one tribe has worshipped one God and their neighbouring tribe has worshipped another. Now, Christ is

> ### What Saint Athanasius Said
>
> "So the human being, henceforth closed in on every side and seeing everywhere, that is in heaven, in hell, and in the human being, the divinity of the Word unfolded over the earth, he is no longer deceived concerning God, but reveres Him alone, and through Him rightly knows the Father."

worshipped in all places; they all praise the one and the same Lord and through Him His Father.

WHAT THE SCRIPTURES SAY:

"For the message of the cross is foolishness to those who are perishing, but to us who are being saved it is the power of God. For it is written: "I will destroy the wisdom of the wise and bring to nothing the understanding of the prudent." Where is the wise? Where is the scribe? Where is the disputer of this age? Has not God made foolish the wisdom of this world? For since, in the wisdom of God, the world through wisdom did not know God, it pleased God through the foolishness of the message preached to save those who believe. For Jews request a sign, and Greeks seek after wisdom; but we preach Christ crucified, to the Jews a stumbling block and to the Greeks foolishness, but to those who are called, both Jews and Greeks, Christ the power of God and the wisdom of God. Because the foolishness of God is wiser than men, and the weakness of God is stronger than men." 1 Corinthians 1:18-24

[47]. From early times, men have been led astray and worshipped springs or rivers, wood or stone and have thought them gods. Men have worshipped Zeus and Chronos, Apollo and the heroes and thought them gods too. But by the sign of the cross, they are shown to be demons or simply men no different from the rest. Magic filled the

world and astonished the Egyptians, the Chaldaeans, and the Indians but when at the time of the manifestation of the Word of God, when Christ the Wisdom of the Father appeared, that was proved wrong and utterly destroyed.

Now St Athanasius asks us to look at those men who have been responsible for sharing the teachings of the Greeks and of Christianity. Famous philosophers like Socrates and Plato were full of wisdom and had fine tongues, yet what do they have to show for it? They failed even to convince their neighbours of the immortality of the soul and how to live the virtuous life. Yet, Christ chose the lowly and the modest, He chose those of

REFLECTION

God chose the weak and the simple and turned the world on its head. Power was shown not in subjecting others to your control, but in being their servant; not in killing others, but in dying for others; not in pride and power but in humility and love. Do I remember that Christ has overcome the world and its teachings? Do I remember to be a servant and not a tyrant? Do I remember to be humble and loving, and not proud?

"So then, if the Saviour is not simply a human being, nor a magician, nor a demon, but by His divinity has destroyed and overshadowed the suppositions of poets and the illusions of the demons and the wisdom of the Greeks, it should be clear and will be confessed by all that this one is the true Son of God, being the Word and Wisdom and Power of the Father. For this reason, His works are not human, but beyond human, and they are known to be truly of God both from the very appearances and by comparison with those of human beings"

simple words and those considered unwise according to human standards, and yet His teachings fill the world. Man, with Christ's guidance, has turned from temporal things to things eternal, from being fearful of death to trampling on it, from earthly glory to divine immortality.

[48]. We have seen all these things: that Christ casts out demons and makes magic foolish and is far more powerful despite man's weakness than the teachings of the Greeks may suggest. Who then is this Christ? What manner of person must He be? St Athanasius asks this to the Greeks and anticipates what kind of responses they will give. Will they call Him a magician? But surely a man who destroys magic is far more powerful than it and cannot be fitly described as a magician. Is He a demon? But the same argument is true, and St Athanasius invites us to test: merely performing the sign of the cross will make any demon flee [if you are too afraid to try it, simply ask the monks]. Surely, He is not then a demon. The Pharisees said the very same thing and Christ Himself ridiculed the idea.

Who then is He who has this power, a power that is greater than nature? He can be nothing else than the Son of God, the Word and Wisdom and Power of the Father. Surely the most reasonable response is this, for no other account of Him and who He is and where He is from can describe Him as well as this.

[49]. St Athanasius compares the works of Christ with some of the works of the Greek gods. First up is Asclepios. He was made a god by the Greeks because he practiced healing and discovered herbs which were cures for various ailments of man. But these are simply the accomplishments of science. Christ Himself made one born blind see, and restored creation to its proper state, which is a far greater accomplishment.

Next is Heracles (or Hercules), who is worshipped by the Greeks for his great strength who fought with humans equal to himself and killed wild beasts. But what does that compare to Christ, who helped human beings instead of fought with them and made His enemies the demons and sicknesses and even death itself?

Last is Dionysius, a god of drunkenness and partying. He taught humanity drunkenness and they mock Christ who taught sobriety. But let these things be, for their drunkenness blinds them from Christ's other great works: the sun was darkened, and the world shook at His death and He rose from the dead. No man can boast of such deeds. His worship spreads throughout the world, even to their areas that were once under the domain of other Greek gods and they fail to stop Him. Who is more powerful then He?

[50]. Christ was superior to the Greek deities named above, but what about to other men? St Athanasius asks us, which man of all

the tyrants and kings on the earth before Him has filled the earth with His teaching as Christ has done? Which man has turned away so many people in the world from the vain worship of idols and to Himself? Despite the Greeks' persuasiveness, they fall to their knees when confronted with the cross of Christ. Despite their finely constructed arguments and grand language, they were contested by others through their life and after they died. Yet, as St Athanasius writes, "The Word of God, in the greatest paradox, teaching with poorer words, has cast into the shade the greatest sophists, and reduced to naught their teachings, and by drawing all to Himself has filled His churches."

What is remarkable is that Christ accomplished this in His death. What seemed a great defeat was His finest victory. Through

REFLECTION

St Athanasius focuses on the works of Christ and compares it here with simply the words of the Greeks. Sometimes our actions are far more convincing than any argument. Showing someone Christ's love may be far stronger than showing someone a sound argument. Yet, perhaps because it is much more potent, it is also much harder.

His death and resurrection, He made the adulterers chaste, the murderers drop their swords, and the cowards courageous. Through His death and resurrection, He has offered a far stronger argument for the immortality of the soul than the Greeks could ever conjure with words. Through His death and resurrection, He has shown to all that He is the Son of God, the Wisdom of the Father.

WHAT THE SCRIPTURES SAY:

"Who shall separate us from the love of Christ? Shall tribulation, or distress, or persecution, or famine, or nakedness, or peril, or sword?" (Romans 8:35). Christ has given His love freely to all men. We are to imitate Him.

[51]. Who among humans had such faith in humanity as Christ had? Before Christ, man had looked at the dire state of humankind and thought it almost impossible to reform man and to better him. But Christ gave man virtues and virginity, charity and chastity, that man might better himself. The Greeks had not been bold enough to venture out to reform the barbarian but had left him in his magic and superstitious ways. But the teachings of Christ, spread through His disciples, have (or aimed to have) aided every man without exception. Christ did not wince from the leprous, nor from the savagery or the poor manner of the barbarian. Now His followers do the same and aid them out of the darkness to cast aside their ancestral gods and to worship Christ and through Him to know the Father.

What Saint Athanasius Said

"When they hear the teaching of Christ they immediately turn to farming instead of war, and instead of arming their hands with swords they stretch them out in prayer, and, in a word, instead of fighting amongst themselves, henceforth they arm themselves against the devil and the demons, subduing them with sobriety and virtue of soul."

WHAT THE SCRIPTURES SAY:

"Who shall separate us from the love of Christ? Shall tribulation, or distress, or persecution, or famine, or nakedness, or peril, or sword?" (Romans 8:35). Christ has given His love freely to all men. We are to imitate Him.

[52]. Christ has not considered Himself too great to help the uncultivated barbarians who are constantly given in war and fighting with men. But what is wondrous is that though they have been warlike people and savage in their manners, by the power of the Word of God they have turned their swords into ploughshares. This is an argument for His divinity, St Athanasius says. No idol was ever able to change the hating hearts of these barbarians from hearts of stone to hearts of flesh, but Christ alone was able. What man was not able to learn from the idols, he was able to learn from Christ. The idols, or demons, have always bred discord among the people so that man would turn and fight amongst themselves instead of turning against the demon. Now, by living lives of purity and with their virtues as weapons, man has turned to wage warfare against the demons of this world instead.

WHAT THE SCRIPTURES SAY:

"They will beat their swords into ploughshares and their spears into sickles, and nation shall not lift up sword against nation, neither will they learn any more to wage war." (Isaiah 2:4)

[53]. This points to another argument for Christ's divinity, says St Athanasius. What man in the world's history, be he a magician, a tyrant, or a king, was ever able to take on all the powers of the world – the wisdom of Greek philosophy, the strength and deceit of their idols, and all the demoniacal legion – and yet conquer them all, and to save man from their clutches? What man in the world's history was ever able to show them not only to be wrong, but to be foolish and weak and to strengthen man to trample upon them and to turn to the Gospels above all else? Was there ever a man who existed like our Christ?

Now, man turns away and the wise of this world who spat upon Christ in the past now bow down to worship Him. St Athansius asks, if these are the works of a mere man, then someone should explain to us how this was possible. Surely, if one has power over the universe and all things that are in it, this must be someone divine. This must be God. Our Christ is the Lord of glory, the Saviour of all.

[54]. We are not able to see God, because He is invisible by His nature, but we are able to see His works. If anyone sees the works of Christ, He will surely now – by the arguments St Athanasius has given – be able to see that His works are divine. Let us marvel, then, that the mighty works of God might be done from such a simple creature as man. His glory is all the greater for His humility. Now, through His humility, He has conquered death and

brought incorruptibility to all. Now, the Word of God has been revealed to us and has also revealed to us His Father.

Perhaps the most famous line in the whole book then follows: "For He was incarnate that we might be made god." Or in other words, God became man so that man might become god. What radical language! What an unbelievable generosity and an incomprehensible gift! He endured the greatest shame that we might receive the greatest gift.

While this is one of the greatest of His works, Christ's accomplishments are numerous. St Athanasius says that anyone who wishes to assess the kind and number of His works would be like one who is trying to count the waves: he simply can't, the ones coming on will escape his attention, they are far too many and he can't even look at them

REFLECTION

Sometimes we get angry and don't know how to control it or where to direct it. Perhaps we were given these emotions to turn inward and direct it against the evil and wickedness of our own hearts that we may wage spiritual warfare for the betterment of our souls and bodies. Be faster to pick up a prayer against your vices than a sword against your brother.

all. Importantly, he can't see the whole of them but only some of them at any stage. So it is with Christ's works in the body, one cannot see the whole but only the part which is exceedingly marvellous and so one can only wonder at the whole. Everywhere, Christ's works reveal His divinity and we cannot grasp the whole of it in our simplicity. It is like hugging a mountain.

WHAT THE SCRIPTURES SAY:

"His divine power has given to us all things that pertain to life and godliness, through the knowledge of Him who called us by glory and virtue, by which have been given to us exceedingly great and precious promises, that through these you may be partakers of the divine nature, having escaped the corruption that is in the world through lust." 2 Peter 1:3-4 We are called to be "partakers of the divine nature" through the knowledge of Christ. Just as St Athanasius says, we are to become 'gods' for this is why Christ became man.

[55]. St Athanasius here summarises his argument against the Gentiles (specifically, the Greeks). The wisdom of the Greeks no longer grows and even steadily disappears, the idols and worship of demons no longer spreads but falls. Christ increases everywhere, and everything opposed to Him weakens and perishes. [We should note, as we have before, many of St Athanasius' arguments would be far stronger in his time when Christianity spread with such force. It is to our shame that his arguments do not hold the same strength

What Saint Athanasius Said

"For He was incarnate that we might be made god; and He manifested himself through a body that we might receive an idea of the invisible Father; and He endured the insult of human beings, that we might inherit incorruptibility. He Himself was harmed in no way, being impassible and incorruptible and the very Word and God; but He held and preserved in His own impassibility the suffering human beings, on whose account He endured these things."

as they did and as they should].

St Athanasius describes Christ as like the sun: just as it rises and repels all darkness steadily covering the whole landscape, so too does Christ's teaching illumine the whole world. He is the Light of the world. In another analogy, think of a king who sits in his castle; his subjects grow proud and begin to take advantage of the liberties he has given them, trying to make themselves kings and rulers. But when the king leaves his castle and travels through the land, those same trying to take advantage of him cower and flee. Thus it is with Christ who has conquered the proud among the demons and among human beings who have tried to take the role of god. These things, which are weak and finite, pass away, but Christ endures forever.

REFLECTION

At the heart of Orthodoxy is the call to 'theosis' or 'deification' which means 'to become god'. Be scared by this scary language! We are called not simply to be good, because a simple man can be a good man, but to become god. This is so far out of our reach that it leaves us with no choice but to call out to God in prayer and beg Him to transform us. Only in our humility can we accomplish so great a task.

> ## What Saint Athanasius Said
>
> "For as human
> things cease and
> the word of Christ
> abides, it is clear to
> all that the things
> which cease are
> transient, and He
> who abides is God
> and true Son and
> only-begotten Word
> of God"

REFLECTION

Hinted at in this chapter, some people (and demons/idols) have tried to make themselves god and this is certainly evil. But we could ask, isn't this what St Athanasius said Christ came to do [i.e. He became man so that we might become god]? But the difference is that when you make yourself god, you do it by your own power – the power of one created, the power of one who is by nature not a god. When you approach God in humility and ask Him to change your heart, He can make you a partaker of the divine nature because it is within His power to do so.

CHAPTER VI SUMMARY

What happened in this chapter is as follows:

- Christ appearing in a body is not absurd: He is the maker of the universe and present in all of it, therefore it is not unreasonable that He be present in part

- God could not simply save man with a nod of the head without destroying man; He had to destroy corruption which had become part of the body

- That Christ is divine, is declared by the state of the world since He has come: the demons cease, Greek wisdom perishes, and His word spreads throughout the world

- God became man so that man might become god

CHAPTER SEVEN

CONCLUSION

What Saint Athanasius Said

"You will also know of His second glorious and truly divine manifestation to us, when He comes no longer in lowliness but in His own glory, no longer with humility but in His own magnificence, no longer to suffer but to bestow thenceforth the fruit of His own cross on all – I mean the resurrection and incorruptibility – no longer judged, but judging all according to what each one has done in the body, whether good or evil, whence there is laid up for the good of the kingdom of heaven, but for them that have done evil, eternal fire and outer darkness."

[56]. St Athanasius now begins to conclude the book (or letter). These arguments and this picture he has painted, he says, is just an "elementary sketch", just the beginning of a far larger story, of a much bigger gallery. To know more, we must read the Bible and read it genuinely applying our mind to it for these writings were spoken and written by God. Knowing these things, we will be ready to see and receive Christ when He comes again in His glory. We will be ready to stand before the "judgment seat of Christ" (2 Corinthians 5:10). We will be ready to receive His gift, or, God forbid, His punishment.

[57]. But there is something important that we must do to understand the Bible, to understand this book, and to understand any teaching of Christ from Himself or through the Church: we must live a virtuous life. Living a virtuous life and having a pure soul is the greatest guide for the mind so that it can learn about God. St Athanasius writes, "Without a pure mind and a life modelled on the saints, no one can comprehend the words of the saints" – that's the whole Bible and everything ever written authoritatively by the Church. Just as someone, if he wished to see the sun would wipe his eyes, or if someone wished to see a particular city or country, would go to that city or country so too, if someone wishes to learn the mind and the way of the Fathers, the teachings of the theologians, and the

wisdom of Christ, he "must first wash and cleanse his soul by his manner of life." Only by preparing his heart, can a man's mind amount to anything. Only by preparing in this way can a man receive that "which eye has not seen, nor ear heard, nor has entered into the heart of man" (1 Corinthians 2:9). Only by preparing one's whole being can a man receive the things prepared by God the Father in Christ Jesus our Lord, "through whom and with whom, to the Father with the Son Himself in the Holy Spirit, be honour and power and glory to the ages of ages. Amen."

Though now we have finished arguably St Athanasius' greatest work, we end on a humble note that we should never forget: a single act of loving kindness is far greater than all the books in the world.

What Saint Athanasius Said

"One wishing to comprehend the mind of the theologians must first wash and cleanse his soul by his manner of life, and approach the saints themselves by the imitation of their works, so that being with them in the conduct of a common life, he may understand also the things revealed to them, and thenceforth, as joined to them, may escape the peril of the sinners and their fire on the day of judgement."

CPSIA information can be obtained
at www.ICGtesting.com
Printed in the USA
FFHW021912161219
57032213-62633FF